ALLISON MILLER

✓ Have we **wondered** how Facebook could **transform** into business?

✓ **Secret of Fast & Easy Marketing** tools

✓ **Kick** start with business with **zero stock**

✓ **Steps by steps** with easy guide on business page

✓ Facebook as **ATM**

✓ **Expansion** of business on Facebook

✓ **Instant & two way** Connection with audio & visual

✓ **Receive Money**

CONTENT

1. Have we wondered how Facebook could transform into business?

2. Secret of Fast & Easy Marketing tools

3. Kick start with business without a product and logistic burden

4. Steps by steps with easy guide on business page

5. Facebook as ATM

6. Expansion of business on Facebook

7. Instant & two ways Connection with audio and visual

8. Receive Money via paypal, cheque bank transfer

Initially, I thought Facebook is just a channel for us to connect to our friends, family, colleague and ex-colleague from around the world.

Suddenly, one day I was curious could we transform our Facebook into business as there are so many people there. Currently, we have 800 million users from Facebook.

Wow I saw this cakes, I was really hungry almost feel like wanted to eat a piece from it. Imagine if we could build business with this big cake pool. Isn't it amazing…

It is logic as most of us on Facebook, what about Gen X, Y and Z?

1. Have we wondered how Facebook could transform into business?

It is simple. There are many ways to transform Facebook into business. It depends on whether we want to DIY were own business page or we want to engage an expertise or we want to purchase software to do this or attend SEMINAR to learn this.

If we want to DIY our own business page we may visit the following help from Facebook.

i. http://www.facebook.com/help/pages#!/help/387719477954111/
ii. YouTube
iii. Google

Then, we wonder why we need to transform our Facebook into business page if we already have full time job or business. We are perfectly right. However, do we know nothing is called permanent secure so to create a back-up plan is good.

We all fully aware we are in new era, which is in the fast pace technological golden age. In short we may be replaced by system, internet, and robot.

However, how do we fully utilize this so that we could gain our earning security?

The below is my Facebook fan page.

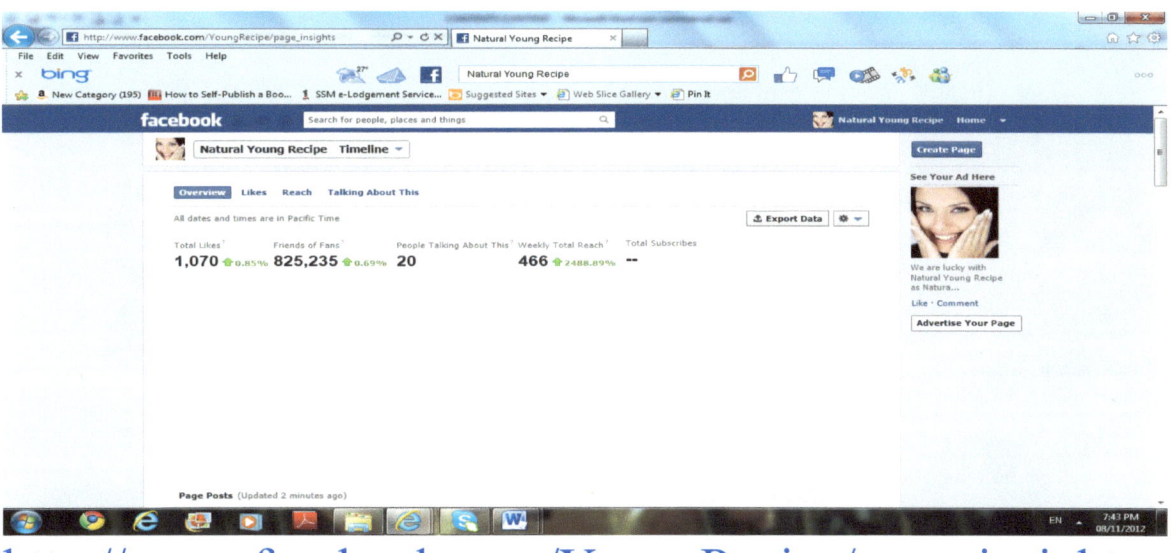

http://www.facebook.com/YoungRecipe/page_insights

I am just an ordinary person like you and me.

How I did this?

The Secret is when I have leisure time I just DIY & go to SEMINAR & Workshop & online training in order to build this.

Due to the unemployment rate is high and I lost my income. I am really thankful that at least these keep me going.

a) Own network

The easiest is start from our own network then expand gradually. Now we may start in the most relaxing manner as we just get connected to our circles by the way business…Find something good or economical to share..

b) Friend's network, family, relatives, colleagues, ex-colleagues

When we have something good we normally share with our family, relatives, friends, colleagues, ex-colleagues. They would be very happy to own that and recommend it for us too.

c) Advertise in Facebook

Facebook is very user friendly as it provides all useful guides for us to refer.

We may refer to the link below for detail guide.
http://www.facebook.com/advertising?campaign_id=217255663720&placement=exact&creative=14339980712&keyword=advertise+in+facebook&extra_1=04b1e749-0cde-de88-ab6b-00000e51a6b7

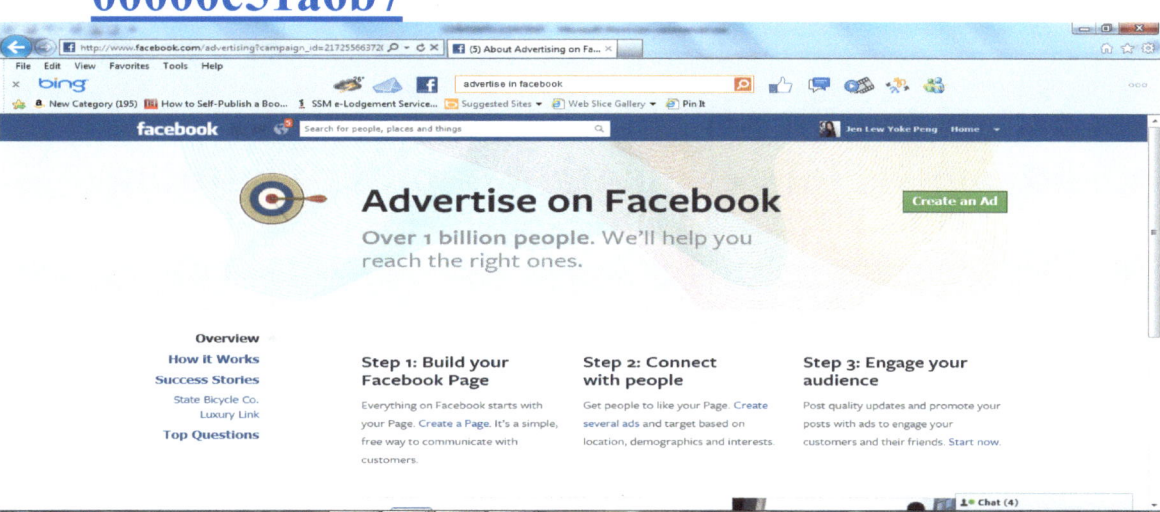

d)Advertise in YouTube

We use to wonder do we need to pay to advertise on YouTube. How others did that? Why they have so many likes and so popular?

Then, I Google most YouTube like…oic… When we have popular key words then when we feel bore we just Google what's up in the YouTube.

We may build our own YouTube channel too. We may visit the following link
http://support.google.com/youtube/?hl=en-GB
Therefore, when we build our channel we may use the popular key word and interesting or funny content to attract visitors.

You may mix with the popular youtube to attract visitors & mention popular youtube channel in our youtube.

e) Twitter

Everyone was so excited with the twitter when an Election happens in US.

With the twitter thy just retweet this reflects by using twitter a brand can use the network to start conversations with followers in advance of promotions when

By posting the link or promotion to twitter the content marketers could gain huge social media market share..

How to create twitter?

Good question, you may visit the link below to guide you there.
http://support.twitter.com/articles/76460-how-to-use-twitter-lists

2. Secret of Fast & Easy & Free Marketing tools

We would be very surprise as entrepreneur also engages with the Facebook to do their marketing.

Facebook allow us to invite our entire network for events. They could join as they like.

When we post page on the timeline it will appear instantly to our network and catch their attention. Normally, they trust us as we are in their network.

Besides, an attractive profile picture and name would attract people attention to join us even they do not even know who are we.

We may use NOTES in the Facebook with picture to share our products or services to them.

We could communicate privately with our Network so nobody could see the private message.

The share function in the Facebook allows us to share post to our network.

I use to pay a lot of attention on the insight to know how attention may I catch in my Facebook fan page.

It is amazing when we see the no. is increasing like rocket. Then I use app from the Facebook to post my promotion there so that I could earn the commission.

We may think how we receive the payment? Stay tune… later I would introduce some ways we could receive payments.

We have to update our status with picture so that our network aware about our business & products.

The words are simple and relaxing in order to catch the network easily.

3. Kick start with business without a product and logistic burden

We are wondering how to start a business without a single product? It is possible. It is normal that everyone need to pay attention to their own business and job. It is time consuming for us to distribute products and services if we already have business and job. How could we do that?

Here is the **SECRET** sell with **ZERO stocks**!!

All the systems/administrative is done by others; once the product is sold you just need to receive the cheque or money in the bank.

We like this ideas right?

We may sign up the affiliate program from Amazon.com or travel agent or click bank or even Tesco who offer the affiliate program. However, we need to have URL. Luckily, Facebook also provide us with URL. However, the best advice is developing our own website. For instance, I have web site www.naturalyoungrecipe.com.

www.naturalyoungrecipe.com

The affiliate program business owner will guide us through in the web site.

What we like the most is to get commission from that business depends on the sales make and the terms and condition offer by those business.

We need to have business page & website in order to add the Promotion items from that business owner.

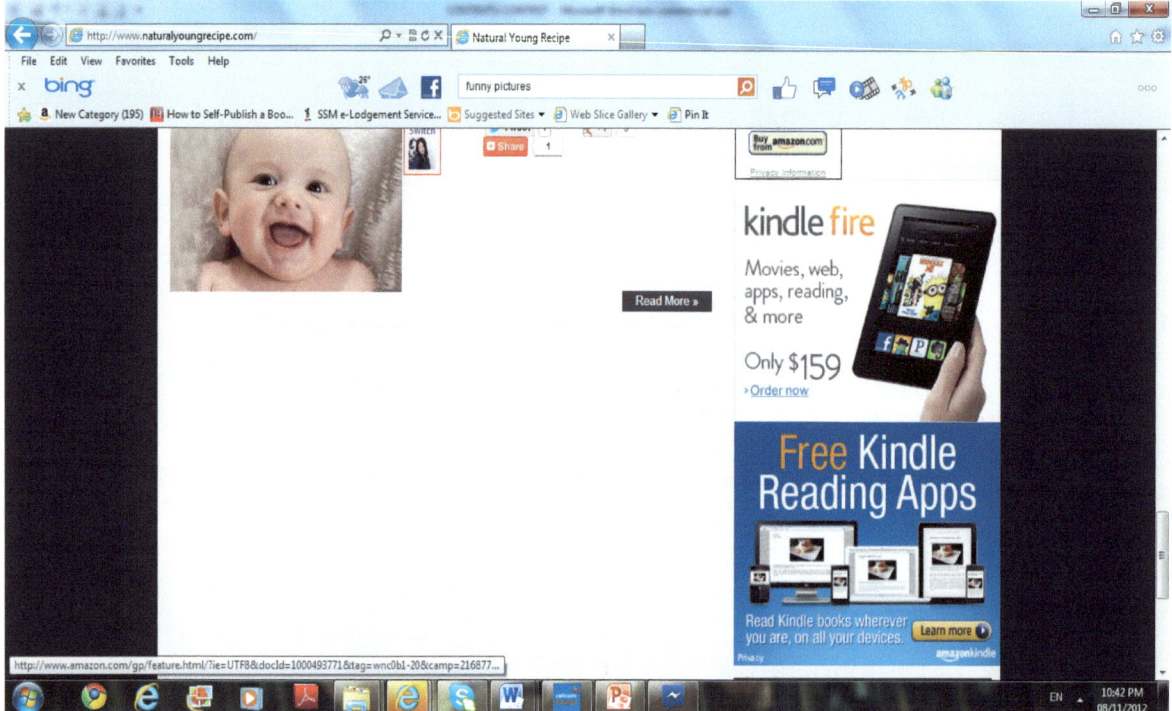

The above is from my web site.
www.naturalyoungrecipe.com

The above is from my facebook fan page
http://www.facebook.com/YoungRecipe#!/YoungRecipe/app_180810088654561

NOW, we just want to start with our Facebook business page instantly right.

If we have our own product & service we may promote there too. Then, we could earn the profits. However we may need to have system and people work for us to despatch the products and deliver the services.

4. Steps by steps with easy guide on business page

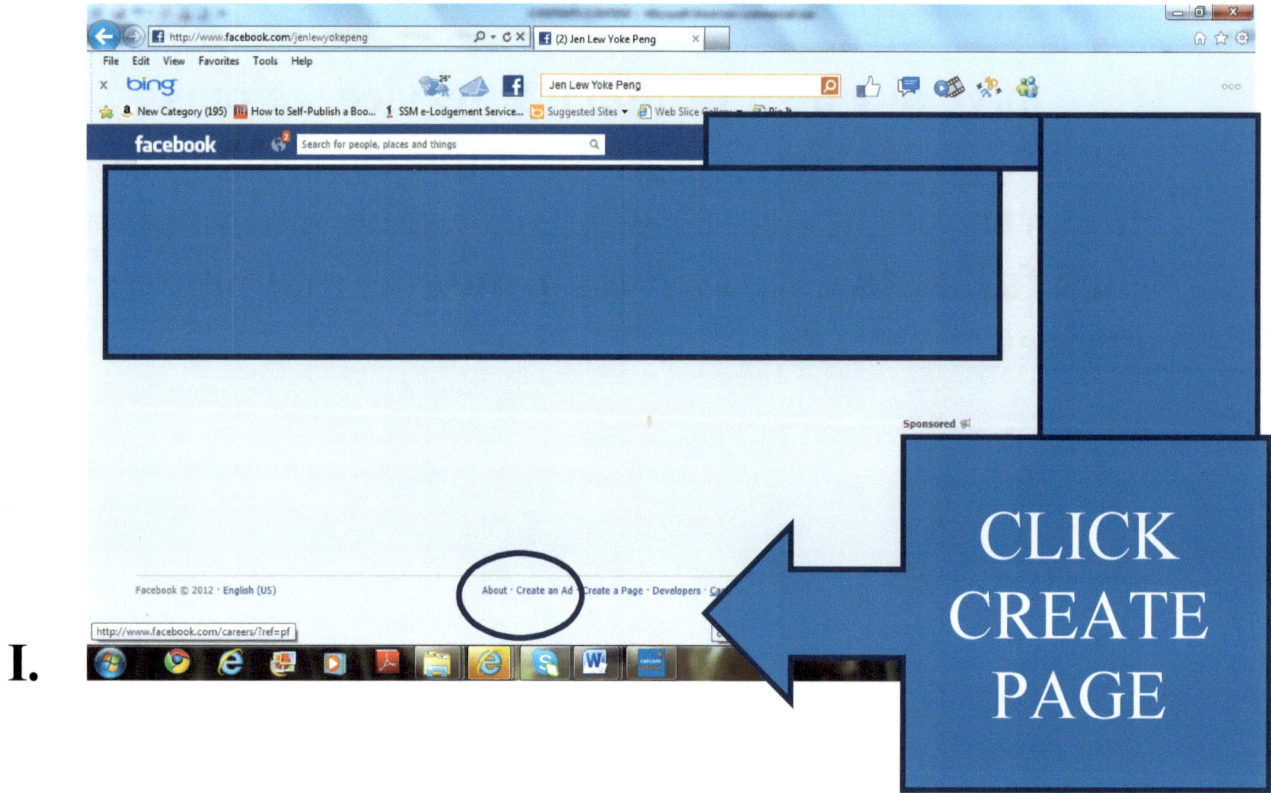

I.

II.

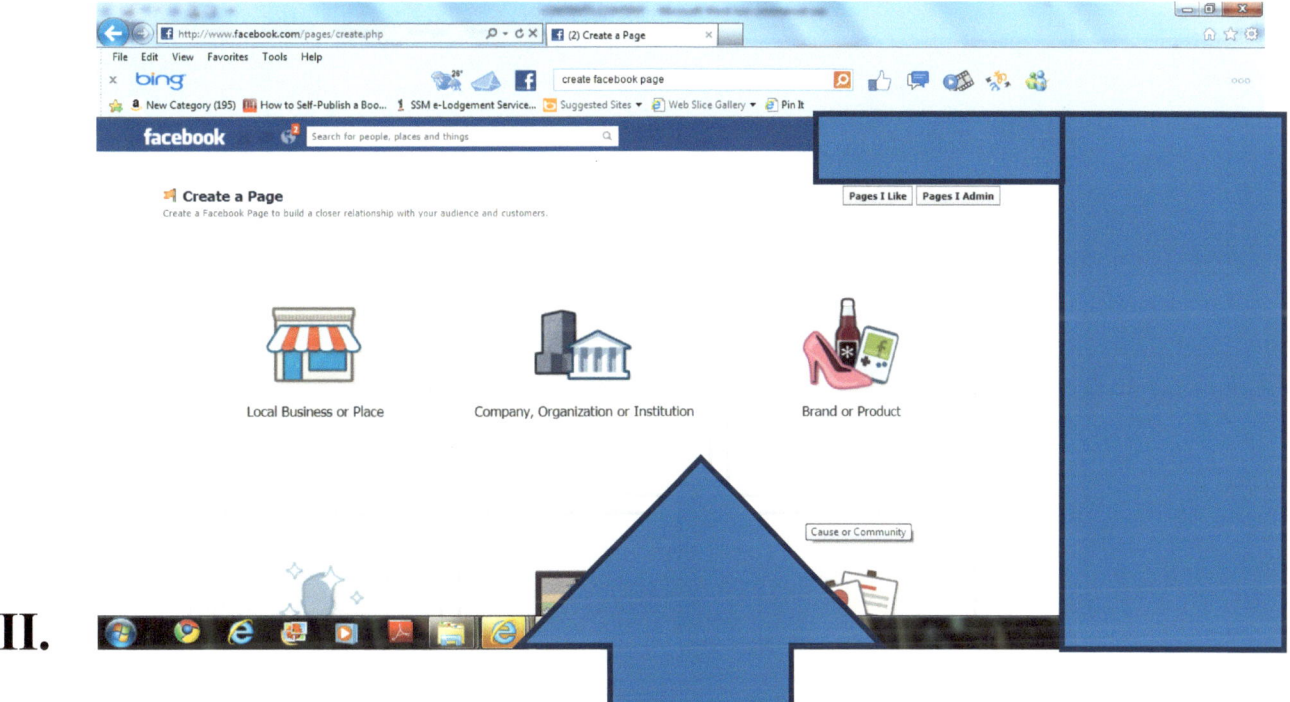

1. CLICK WHICH TYPE OF BUSINESS PAGE YO LIKE.

2. I CHOOSE BRAND BUTTONN

III.

WE MAY CHOOSE THE CATEGORY THAT SUITE OUR BUSINESS.

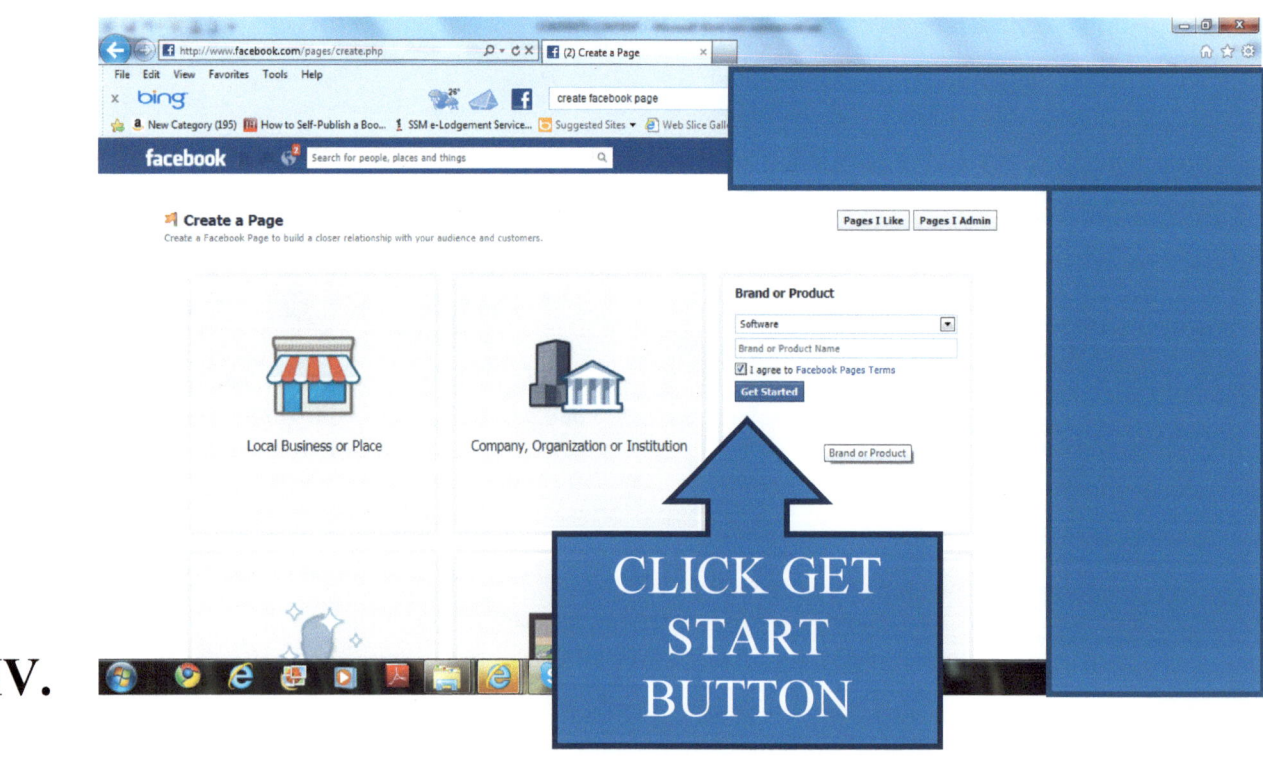

IV.

CLICK GET START BUTTON

V.

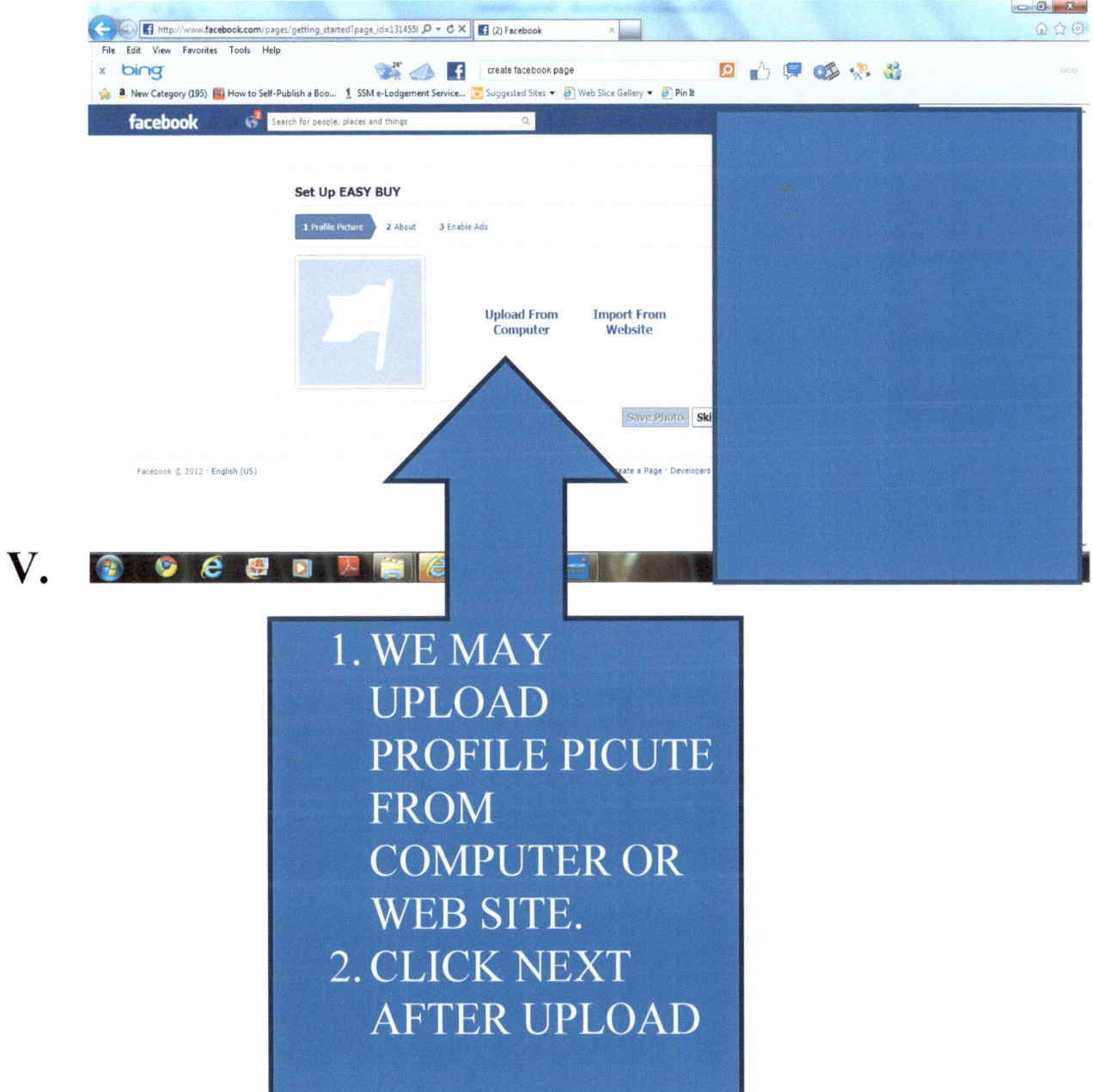

1. WE MAY UPLOAD PROFILE PICUTE FROM COMPUTER OR WEB SITE.
2. CLICK NEXT AFTER UPLOAD

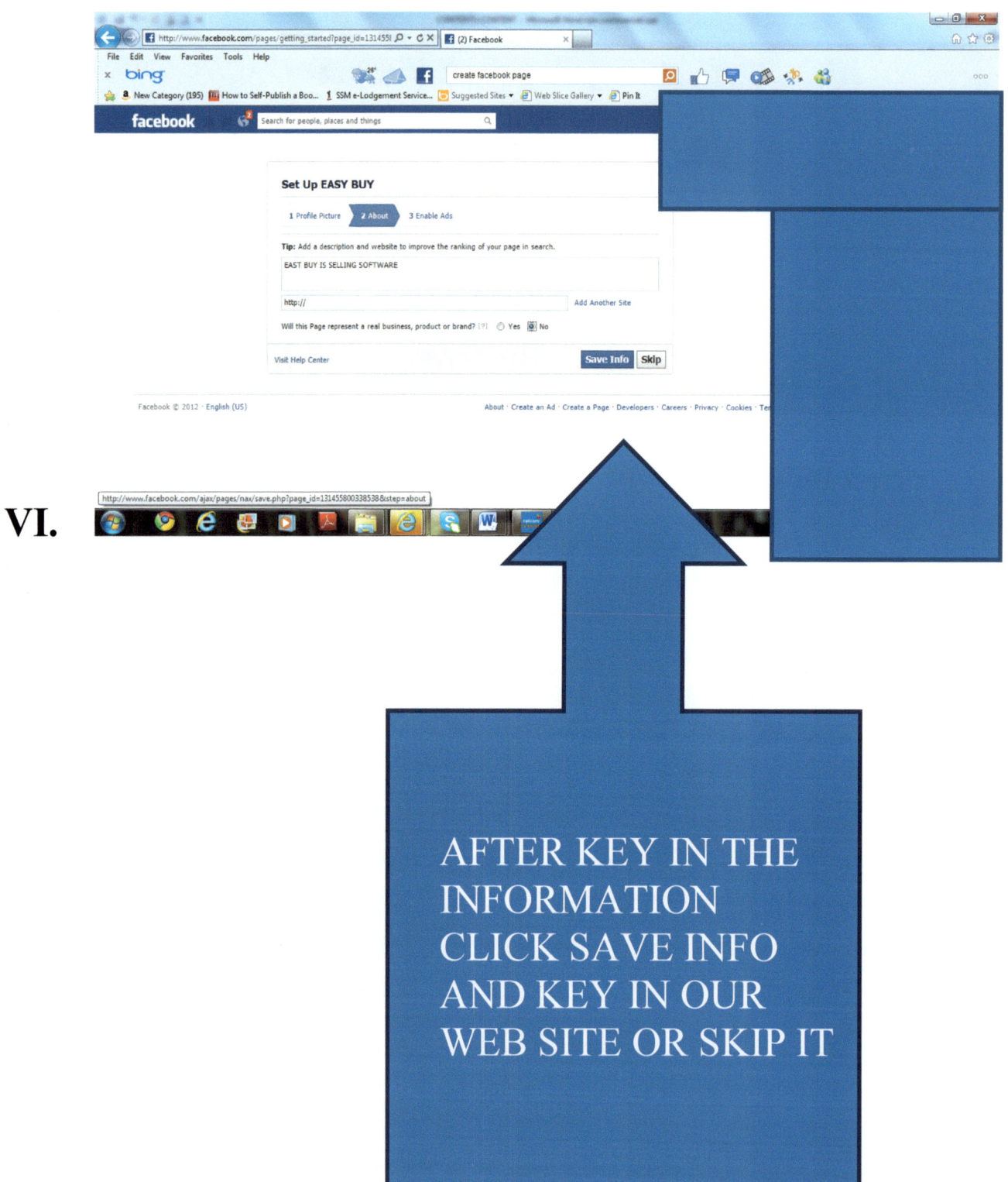

VI.

AFTER KEY IN THE
INFORMATION
CLICK SAVE INFO
AND KEY IN OUR
WEB SITE OR SKIP IT

VII.

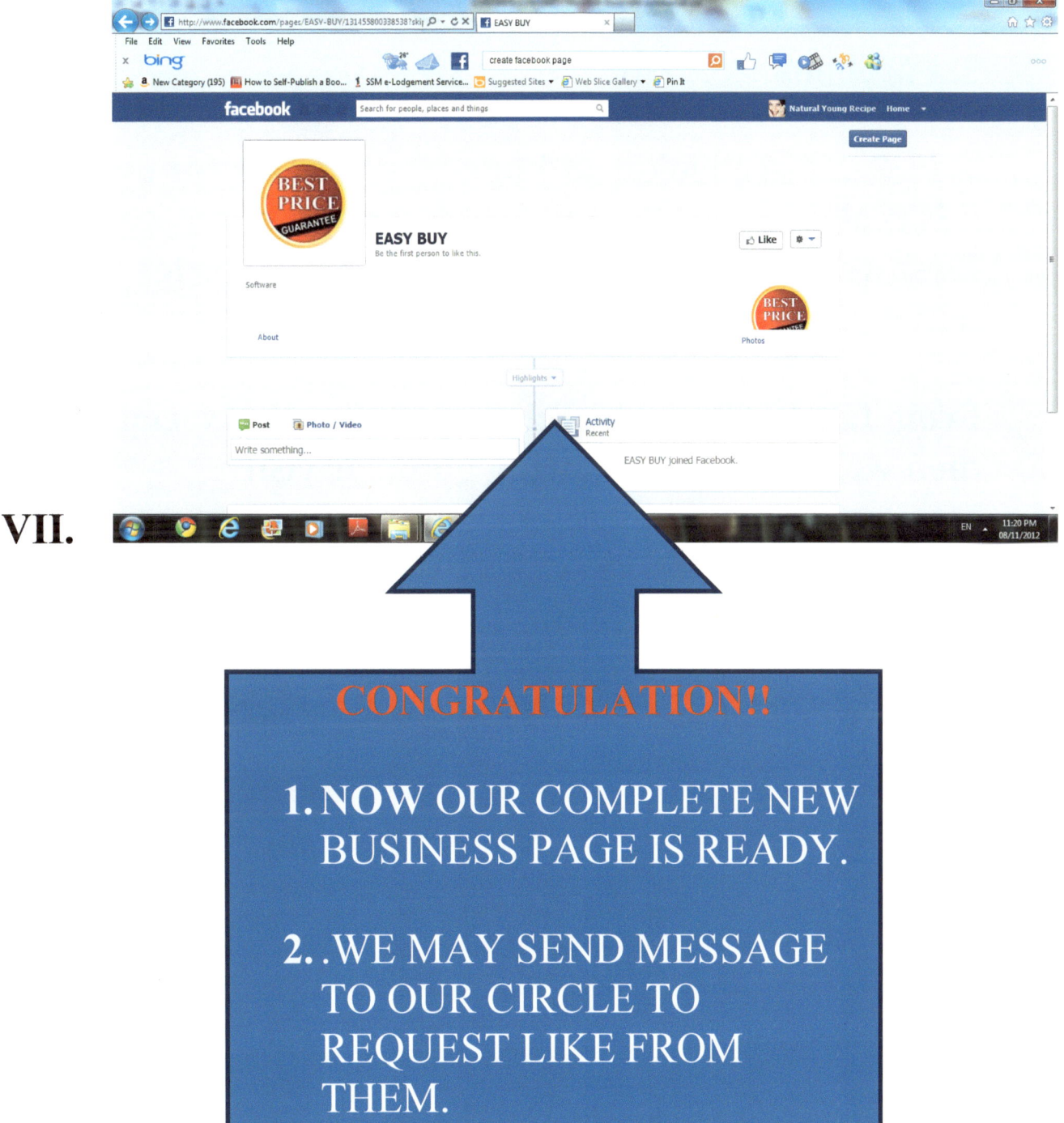

CONGRATULATION!!

1. **NOW** OUR COMPLETE NEW BUSINESS PAGE IS READY.

2. .WE MAY SEND MESSAGE TO OUR CIRCLE TO REQUEST LIKE FROM THEM.

5. Facebook as ATM

WOW… **Facebook could be ATM.** **That is funny yet it is real.**
First we need to choose a facebook app in order to follow the below guidance.

From facebook you search for vendorshop social then we follow the following guide or visit
http://www.vendorshopsocial.com/faqs/

We may start selling now.

How we collect our CASH?

HOW TO CREATE FACEBOOK SHOP

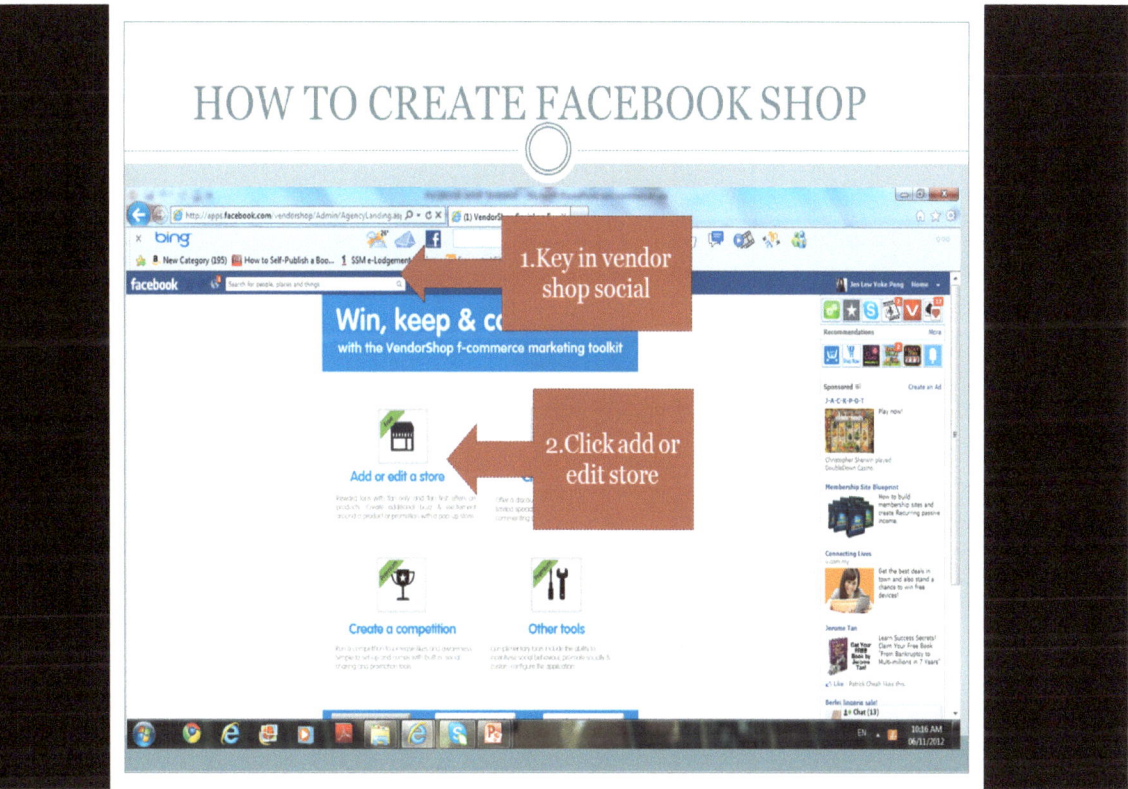

I.

FOLLOW THE FOLLOWING STEP

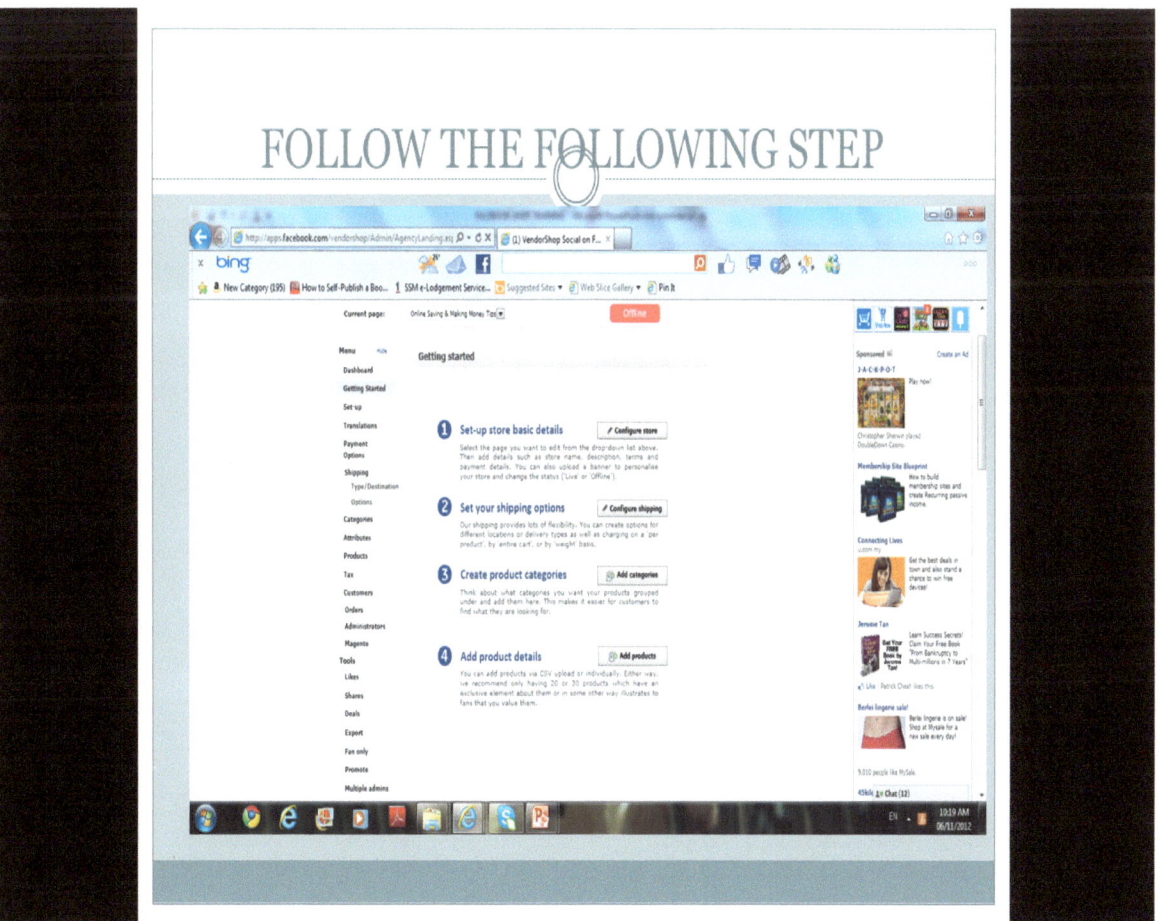

INPUT YOUR INFORMATION

SELECT SHIPPING TYPE

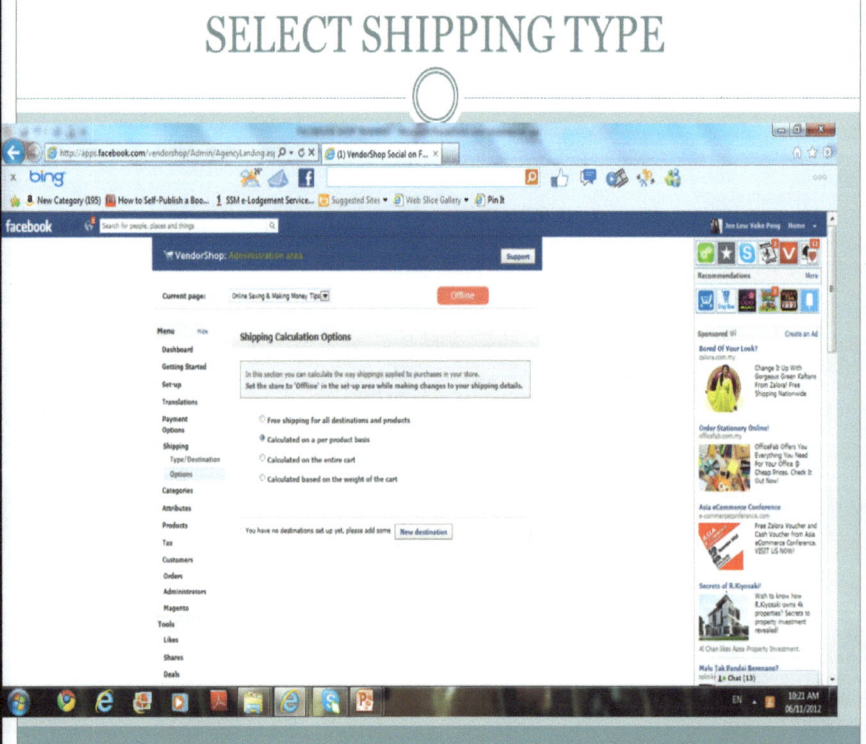

CLICK NEW CATEGORY

KEY IN CATEGORY INFO

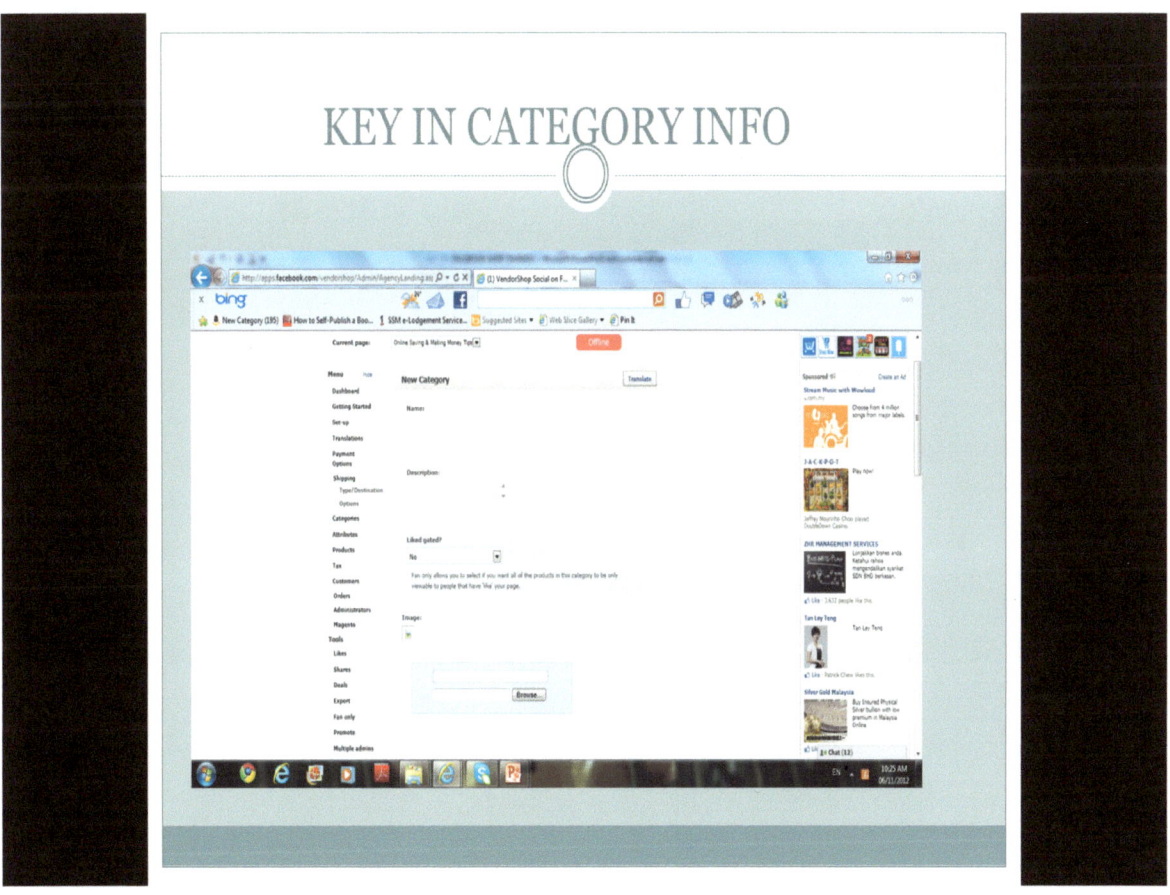

CLICK ADD PRODUCT DETAILS

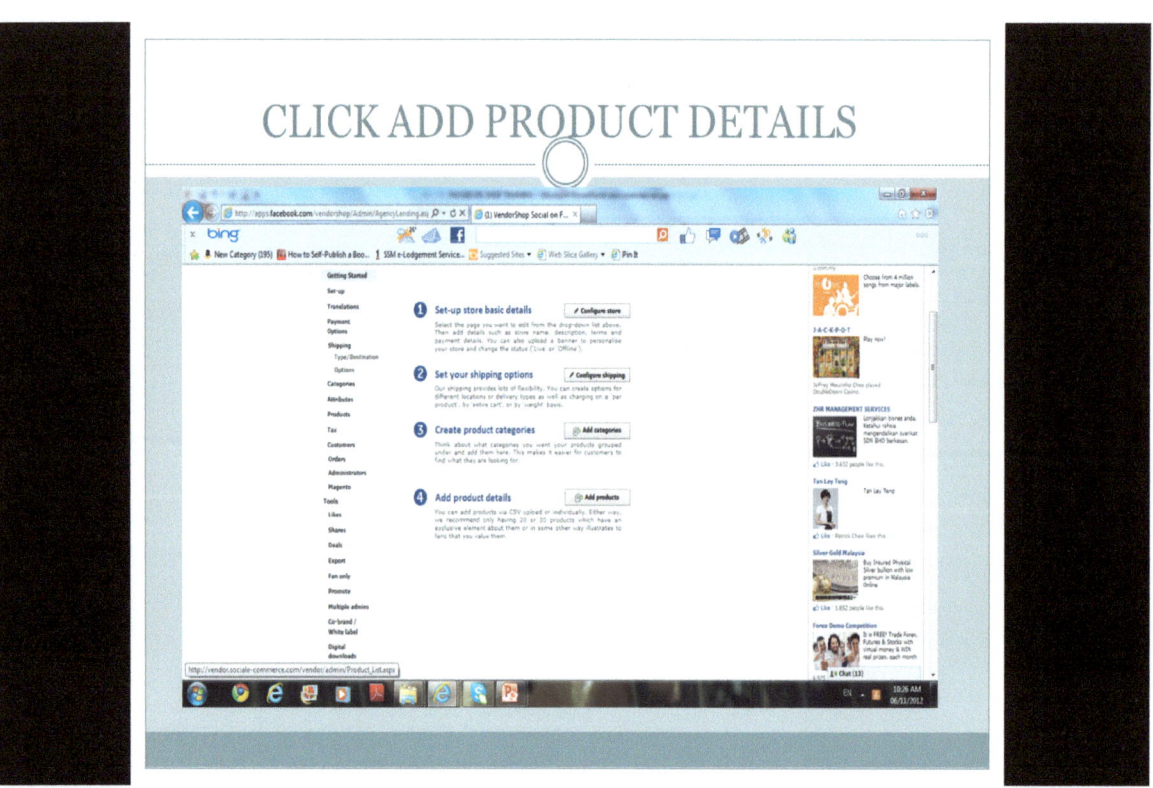

CLICK NEW PRODUCT

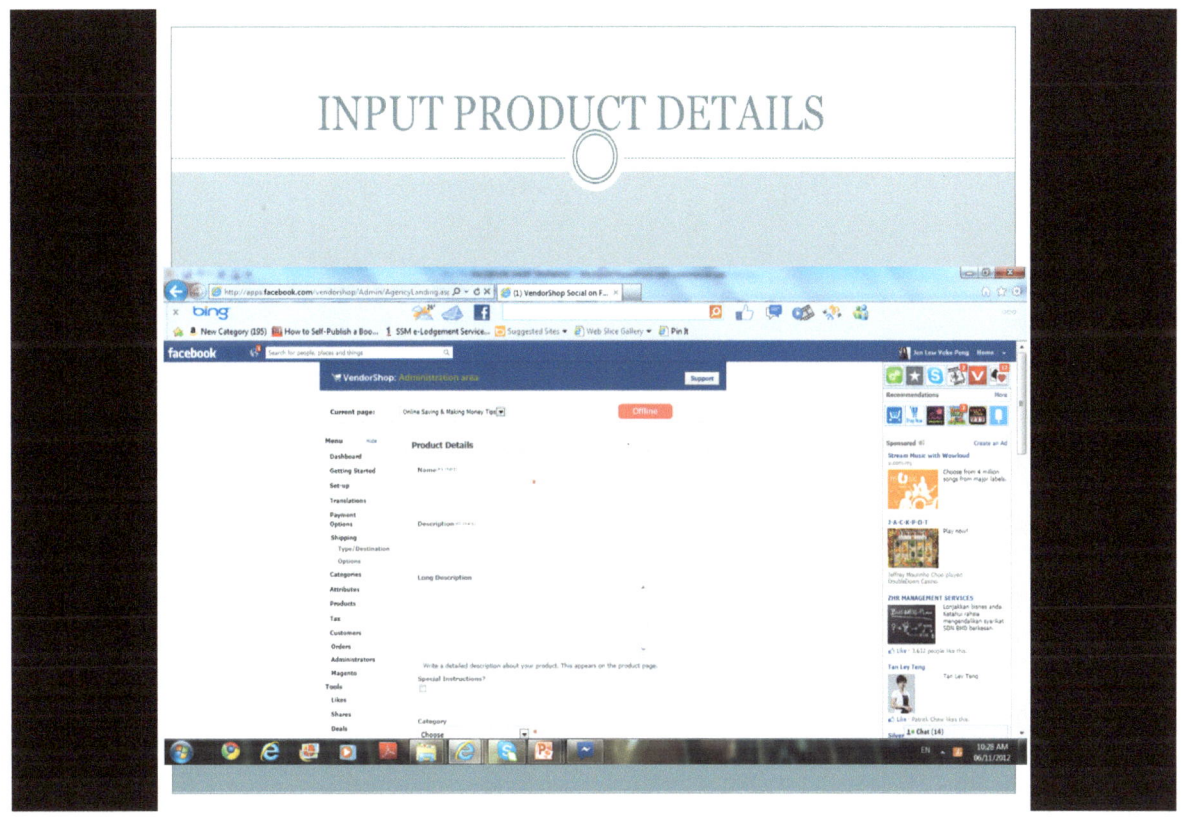

6. Expansion of business on Facebook

We may create another branch on our Facebook shop too. It depends on what we want to sell. It could be clothing, bags, watches etc.

One person could own many shops. Wow I feel very excited with all my shops….

Personally, I have 11 Facebook shop. We may set up the Facebook shop depends on the business nature.

Let's look at the following example is my Facebook shop at http://www.facebook.com/pages/EASY-

BUY/131455800338538?skip_nax_wizard=true#!/YoungRecipe

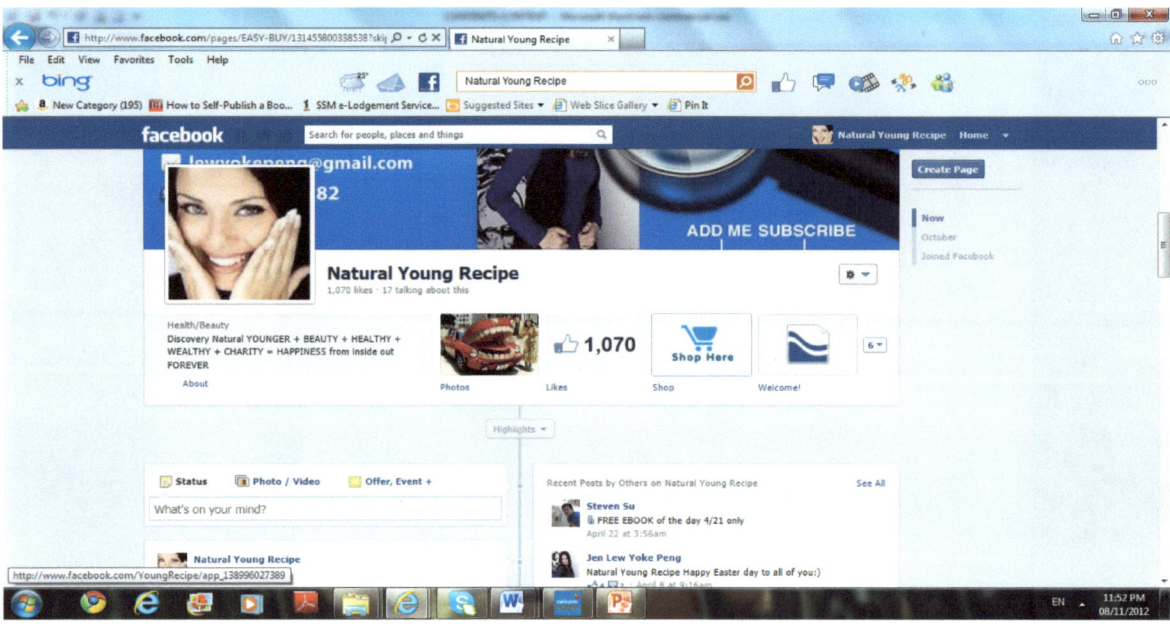

7. Instant & two ways Connection with meeting and talking in group.

In the modern day's business, two way communications is really important. With Facebook we could invite the audience to the events that we organise.

We wonder why we like so much about Facebook, it is all about we could reach too many potential audience and we could communicate with them via messenger or comments or even via skype.

Below is the top fan page in the Facebook. We may visit the following website to view to find our

favourite fan page.

http://fanpagelist.com/category/top_users/

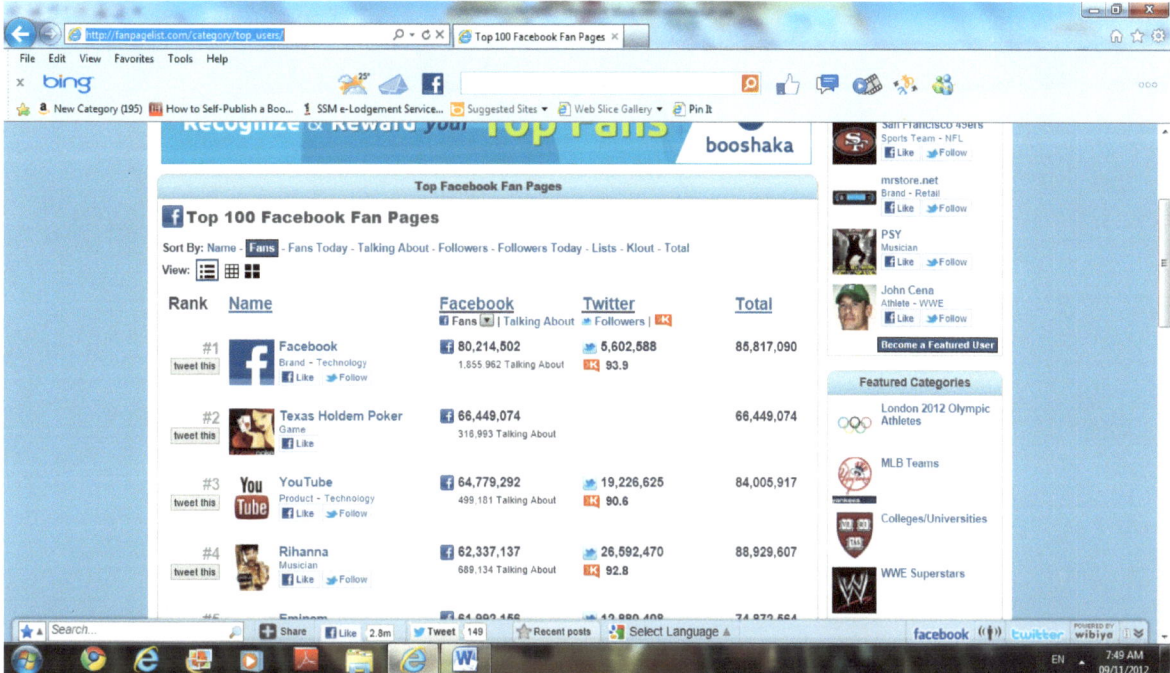

We may download the skype link with the FACEBOOK so we could talk and see the audience if we want to.

The following is the guide to talk and see them at the same time.

http://apps.facebook.com/skype/?fb_source=bookmark_apps&ref=bookmarks&count=0&fb_bmpos=4_0

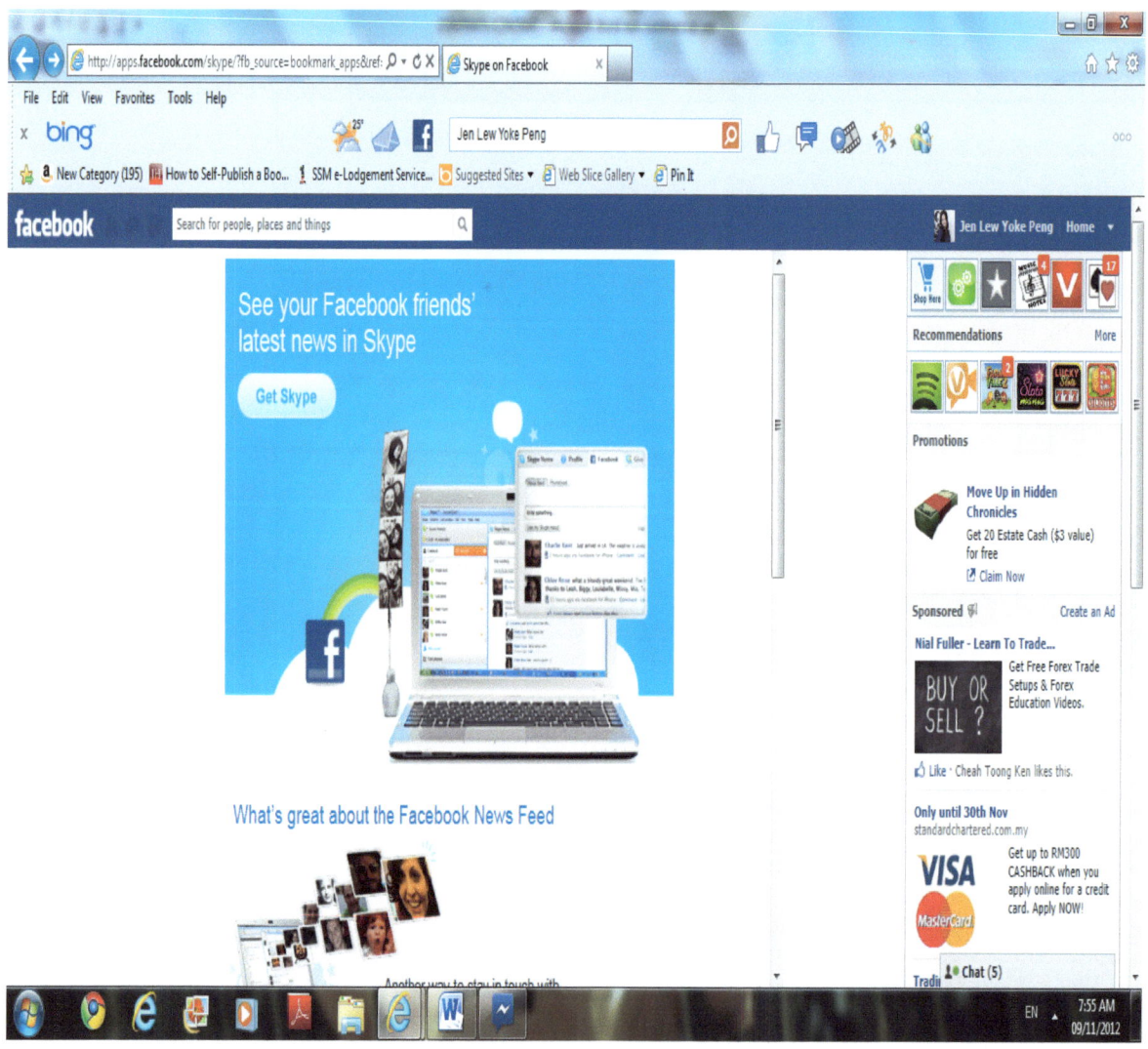

By following the below steps you would be able to get our Skype successfully.

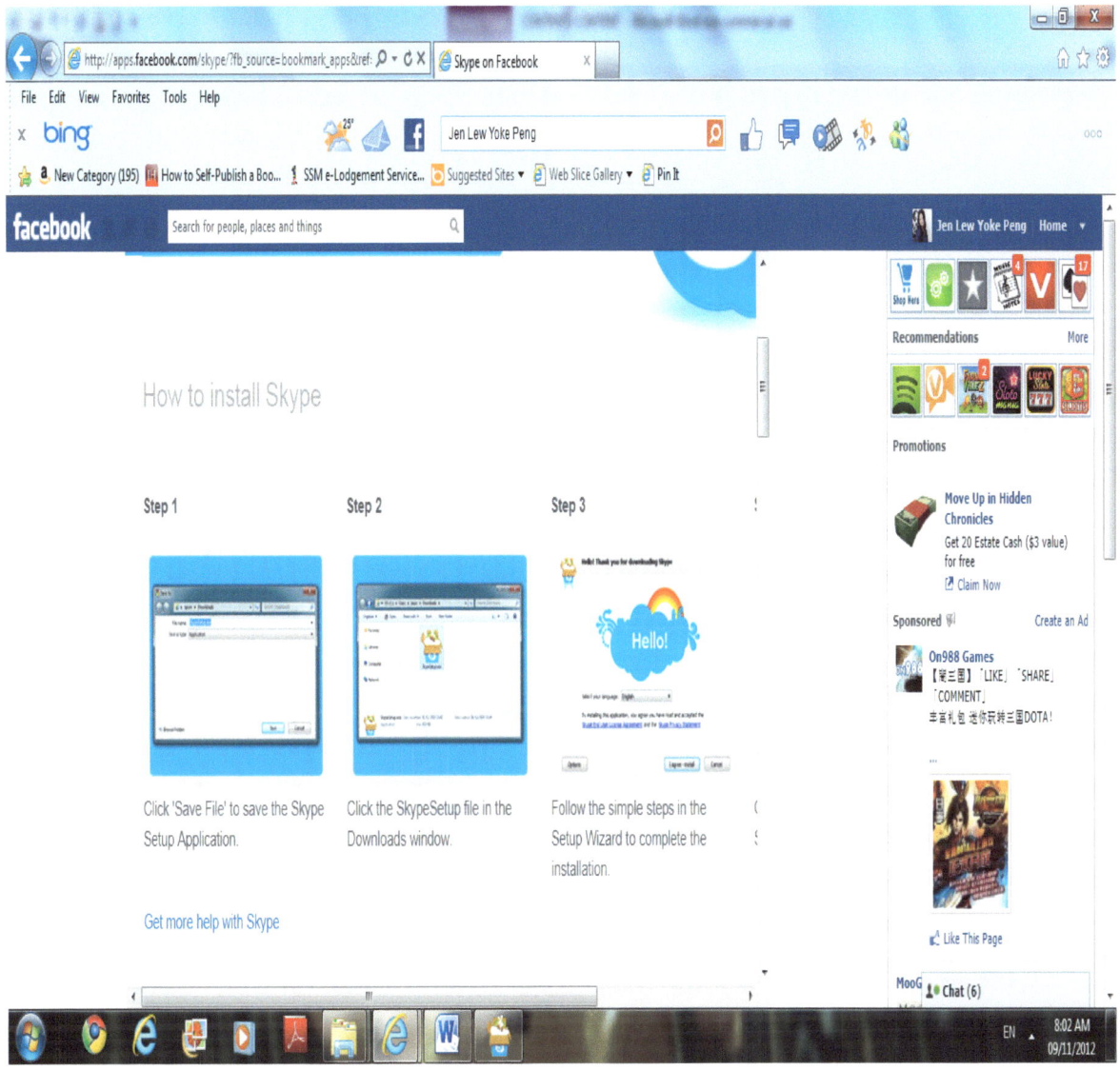

Congratulation!! as you could have audio and visual at the same time with our entire circle.

8. Receive Money via paypal, cheque bank transfer

We use to wonder how to receive money from the audience who interested in our products.

It is easy; we need to sign up with PayPal account just like we sign up our Facebook account with the following link https://www.paypal.com/cy/cgi-bin/webscr?cmd=_home&litebox.x=true

We may follow their step by step guide until our paypal is fully activated.

Why paypal? We just collect cash and put in our paypal pool we could receive our CASH in the paypal and withdrawal whenever we like.

In actual fact paypal can be used in many other businesses with web page.

Why Facebook could be our convenient store?

The answer is because with an app like vendorshop social we could open our shop virtually with ZERO rentals, maintenance fees.

My dear friends, Hope we all have wonderful business page!!